MEGAFAST
MOTORCYCLES

Thanks to the creative team:
Senior Editor: Alice Peebles
Designer: Lauren Woods and collaborate agency

Hungry Tomato™
A division of Lerner Publishing Group, Inc.
241 First Avenue North
Minneapolis, MN 55401 USA

For reading levels and more information, look up this title at www.lernerbooks.com.

Main body text set in Economica Bold.
Typeface provided by Tipotype.

Library of Congress Cataloging-in-Publication Data

The Cataloging-in-Publication Data for *Megafast Motorcycles* is on file at the Library of Congress.

ISBN 978-1-4677-9364-3 (lib. bdg.)
ISBN 978-1-4677-9583-8 (pbk.)
ISBN 978-1-4677-9584-5 (EB pdf)

Manufactured in the United States of America
1 – VP – 12/31/15

MEGAFAST
MOTORCYCLES

by John Farndon
Illustrated by Mat Edwards and Jeremy Pyke

HUNGRY
TOMATO™

CONTENTS

MEGAFAST MOTORCYCLES

The fastest motorcycles today are scarily fast. Most superbikes weigh much less than 500 lb. Yet they are driven by mega-powerful engines that pack a massive punch. Light weight and huge power mean they can accelerate at breakneck speeds. In the hands of a skilled rider, they can typically reach 60 mph in the time it takes you to say Kawasaki Suzuki Honda—that is, under three seconds. And many can roar up to over 200 mph. In this book, we introduce a selection of these motorized beasts…

RECORD BREAKERS

Today's production bikes are so fast that, with just small tweaks, they can be used to set speed records. In 2011, American Bill Warner reached 311.945 mph on a tweaked Suzuki Hayabusa to set the world land speed record for a motorcycle. Sadly, Warner was killed when going for another record in 2013.

RACING ROSSI

Some people think racer Valentino Rossi *(above right)* is the greatest motorcycle rider of all time. He was born in Urbino, Italy, in 1979. His father was a racing motorcyclist too, and Valentino started riding at a very young age. He won his first Grand Prix, on 125cc bikes, at the age of just 17. When the top class MotoGP was introduced in 2002, Rossi won eight of the first nine races. He has since been World Champion six times.

THAT WAS HOW FAST?!

It is easy to see when a plane or a motorcycle, a car or a truck is megafast. But *how* do you know just how fast it is? Speed is the distance that something moves in a certain time. It is the distance covered divided by the time. If a jet plane travels 2,000 miles in two hours, it travels 1,000 miles in each hour. So we say its speed is 1,000 miles per hour, or mph. The top speeds for the machines in this book are given in mph.

SPEED MATTERS

Speeds for vehicles on the ground are typically given in mph (miles per hour) or km/h (kilometers per hour). Rockets may soar away from Earth at over 11 km per second. If a plane flies faster than sound, its speed may be compared to the speed of sound in similar conditions. This speed is called a Mach number. So a plane flying at the speed of sound (typically over 700 mph) is said to be flying at Mach 1.

GETTING QUICKER

One way of seeing how fast something moves is to measure how quickly it gains speed—that is, its acceleration. You can actually measure how much something accelerates every second. But with fast vehicles, the acceleration is usually given by how long it takes to reach a particular speed, typically from a standing start, 0 mph. The shorter the time, the faster the acceleration. So acceleration figures for a superbike that takes just 2.9 seconds to get from a standstill to 60 mph would be 0–60 in 2.9 seconds. That's megafast!

AGAINST THE CLOCK

The most accurate way of measuring top speed is to measure how long a vehicle takes to cover an exact distance, such as a mile. That's how the official top speeds in this book were measured. To ensure split-second accuracy, the clock is triggered to start and stop when the vehicle cuts through a beam of light.

SPEED DIAL

Speed against the clock is average speed. Police speed guns and speedometers in cars, trucks, and motorcycles register the speed at any one instant. Speed guns fire a radar beam and detect the way it bounces off the moving vehicle. With speedometers, an electronic sensor counts the number of times small magnets on the wheel sweep past it each second and converts this into a speed in mph to display on a dashboard or LCD screen.

FLYING TOMAHAWK

The Dodge Tomahawk must be one of the craziest superbikes ever. Dodge claimed its megapowerful engine would slam it up to 420 mph. But no one has ever dared to try it beyond 100 mph. To carry its huge engine, the bike has not two wheels but four. Each can rotate in opposite directions, so the Tomahawk can still lean into bends like other motorcycles.

Top Speed	50	100	200

DON'T MOVE!

The Tomahawk was launched in 2003, but only nine have ever been built. And none can be legally ridden on the road. Dodge says their bike is a "rolling sculpture" and not meant to be ridden seriously. At high speeds a rider will be blown off, as it has no protective fairing!

POWER
500 bhp

0–60 MPH
2.9 seconds

TOP SPEED
420 mph (in your dreams)

ENGINE
8.3 liter, V10 twin-turbocharged

TORQUE
525 lb-ft

PRICE
$550,000

FLYING AX

The Tomahawk gets its name from a kind of ax first used long ago by the native peoples of North America. The original tomahawks had stone heads, but when the Europeans arrived, the stone was replaced with metal blades. Warriors could throw these axes with deadly speed and accuracy.

300   400   500   **420 mph**

KAWASAKI'S NINJA OF THE NIGHT

Kawasaki's H2 Ninja may be the fastest street-legal bike ever. A special supercharged engine forces a mighty 300 hp out of the race version, the H2R. But even the H2 packs a 200-hp punch. In June 2015, rider James Hillier hit an incredible 206 mph on an H2R Ninja on the Isle of Man TT racing circuit, the fastest speed ever achieved there.

BURN-UP

To handle the H2's power, Kawasaki put a lot of technology into the bike's brakes, suspension, and power delivery. The electronic traction-control system adjusts the power delivery to the wheel if it starts to slip when the rider tries to accelerate on a bend.

LEGENDARY NAME

Kawasaki uses the name Ninja for its fastest bikes. Ninjas were spies and assassins in Japanese history. They dressed in dark blue to stay hidden at night and were famous for their speed, stealth, and ability to kill silently. Their skill in climbing and getting into impossible places was legendary. Some said they could even become invisible.

Top Speed | 50 | 100 | 200

POWER
300 bhp

0-200 MPH
5.4 seconds

TOP SPEED
At least 220 mph

ENGINE
998cc supercharged inline-four

TORQUE
1,992 lb-ft max

PRICE
$50,000

300	400	500	2220 mph

SUPERFAST SUZUKI

When Suzuki designed the streamlined shape for the Hayabusa, they were inspired by a swooping bird of prey. The bike they built is a predator of the road, the fastest production motorcycle ever made. Hayabusas made in 1999 and 2000 could reach up to 194 mph! In 2000, though, European and Japanese bike makers agreed to limit road bikes to 186 mph, so this speed can never be bettered.

| Top Speed | 50 | 100 | 200 |

THE FASTEST BIRD

Hayabusa is Japanese for "peregrine falcon." The peregrine dives down on its prey at incredible speeds of 200 mph. That makes it the fastest of all animals. The peregrine also preys on blackbirds--and when it was launched in 1998, the Suzuki Hayabusa chewed up the Honda Blackbird as the world's fastest production bike.

TAME BEAST

Some riders think the Hayabusa is the best superbike ever. It's not just that it's fast--though it is very fast indeed. The bike also handles very nimbly and stably, and it runs remarkably smoothly for such a powerful bike. It's just as at home on city streets as wild mountain roads.

POWER
160 bhp

0-100 MPH
5.3 seconds

TOP SPEED
194 mph

ENGINE
1299cc
inline-four

TORQUE
98 lb-ft

PRICE
About
$12,000

300   400   500

194 mph

15

SHIMMERING LOTUS

When racing car specialists Lotus began building superbikes, they came up with the C-01. With a 200-hp V-twin engine, it's superpowerful, and Lotus calls it a hyperbike. But it's the supersleek carbon "monocoque," or single-shell, body that really catches the eye. It was created by German designer Daniel Simon, who designed the light cycles in the science-fiction movie *Tron*.

Top Speed	50	100	200

FORMULA ONE STYLE

Lotus is one of the most famous names in Formula One (F1) racing cars. In the 1960s and 1970s, famous drivers such as Jim Clark and Graham Hill won race after race in Lotus cars. The design for the C-01 bike was inspired by the Lotus 49 F1 racing car driven by Hill and Clark.

LOTUS FLOWER

The Lotus company was created by racing driver Colin Chapman in 1952. Chapman never said why he chose the name Lotus. Maybe it was his favorite flower. The lotus is sacred in many parts of tropical Asia, where it grows in ponds. Lotus flowers can live over 1,000 years and are a symbol of elegance, beauty, perfection, purity, and grace.

POWER
200 bhp

0-100 MPH
perhaps 5.5 seconds

TOP SPEED
At least 200 mph

ENGINE
1195cc V-twin

TORQUE
168 lb-ft

PRICE
About $137,000

300	400	500	2200 mph

JET-POWERED STORMER

Prepare for takeoff! The MTT Y2K looks like an ordinary motorcycle, but it is powered by a Rolls-Royce M250 jet turbine usually fitted to helicopters. There have been one-off jet-powered bikes propelled by the jet's thrust of hot air alone. But the Y2K's turbine turns a shaft, and the shaft drives the back wheel via a chain, so it can run on the roads just like any other bike. It's just an ordinary bike with extraordinary power.

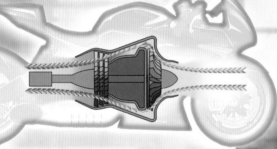

In the Y2K's turboshaft engine, air is swept in the front and squeezed by a fan, mixed with fuel, and set alight by a spark. The burning mix swells rapidly and blasts backwards to turn another fan, turning the shaft that drives the back wheel.

TWO-WHEEL BLAST

When the Y2K was launched in 2000, its performance was terrifying. It could reach 200 mph in just 5.4 seconds. In that time the world's fastest car, the Bugatti Veyron, could only get to 112 mph. An even more powerful version, the MTT Streetfighter, launched in 2008 and can hit over 248 mph.

Top Speed			
	50	100	200

WHAT DOES Y2K MEAN?

Y2K is the millennium or "Year 2 Thousand" (*K* stands for *kilo*, which is Greek for "thousand"), the year that the MTT Y2K was launched. It's best known for the millennium bug or the Y2K bug, which everyone thought would make computers go crazy when midnight came on the last day of 1999. In the end, there were no problems at all.

POWER
420 bhp

0–200 MPH
5.4 seconds

TOP SPEED
248.45 mph

ENGINE
249cc gas turbine

TORQUE
500 lb-ft

PRICE
$200,000

| 300 | 400 | 500 | 248.45 mph |

HONDA HUMDINGER

Honda were annoyed that Kawasaki's Ninja ZX-11 was the world's fastest production bike. They were determined to beat it. And beat it they did with their CBR1100XX Super Blackbird, launched in 1996. For two years the Blackbird was the world's fastest bike, with a rip-roaring top speed of 178.5 mph—until Suzuki fought back with the Hayabusa, which was even faster.

INLINE

Motorcycle engines are identified by their layout and number of cylinders—the tubes in which fuel burns to produce power. The layouts are typically either in a V shape or in a line, most with two or four cylinders. The Honda Blackbird is an inline-four. The cylinders fire in the order 1-3-4-2.

Top Speed

| 50 | 100 | 200 |

JUST LIKE A JET PLANE

The Blackbird is aptly named after the Lockheed SR-71 Blackbird reconnaissance jet of the 1970s. The SR-71 was the world's fastest and highest-flying plane. It could rocket through the air at over 2,193 mph, and in 1974 it roared from New York to London in less than two hours! It could also fly at over 85,000 feet.

POWER
132 bhp

0-60 MPH
3.3 seconds

TOP SPEED
178.5 mph

ENGINE
6.5 liter V12

TORQUE
80 lb-ft

PRICE
About $11,000

300   400   500   **178.5mph**

ELECTRIC LIGHTNING

Lightning's LS-218 is like no other superbike. It's powered not by a gasoline engine but by an electric motor. That means that even at full power there's no throaty exhaust roar—just a quiet whine. And there are no gears to change and no fuel tank, only a battery. But the LS-218 gets its name from its top speed of 218 mph. That makes it one of the fastest road bikes ever.

ALMOST NO MOVING PARTS

Electric motors give the same turning force at all speeds, so there's no need for gears. Twisting the throttle is enough to make the LS-218 go from standstill to top speed. There's little need for brakes either. Twisting the throttle backwards slows down the bike almost as much as brakes would.

LEADING THE CHARGE

The LS-218 doesn't need to fill up with fuel. You just plug it into an electric socket to recharge the batteries. That takes a lot longer than filling up—usually about half an hour. But with no fuel to burn, the LS-218 is much better for the environment than conventional motorcycles.

| Top Speed | 50 | 100 | 200 |

POWER
200 bhp

0-100 MPH
4 seconds

TOP SPEED
218 mph

ENGINE
1.6 liter V6

TORQUE
168 lb-ft

PRICE
$38,888

300   400   500   2218 mph

ON THE FAST TRACK

If you want to go fast on a motorcycle, the best place is on a race track. The fastest races of all are MotoGP, short for Motorcycle Grand Prix. In MotoGP, riders hurtle around flat tracks on purpose-built bikes at speeds of up to 217 mph. They corner at high speeds by leaning far off their bikes to keep them balanced—so far that one knee will scrape the ground!

Top Speed	50	100	200

GOING FOR THE RECORD

MotoGP bikes must conform to strict rules to make sure that riders compete fairly. The maximum permitted engine size is 1,000cc, for example, and the maximum number of cylinders is four. The power output must also be no more than 240 bhp and the top speed no more than 217 mph.

POWER
240 bhp

0–200 MPH
6–7 seconds

TOP SPEED
217 mph

ENGINE
1,000cc

TORQUE
Over 80 lb-ft

PRICE
Unknown

MOTOGP CIRCUITS

In the 2015 season, 18 MotoGP races took place in 13 different countries. There were two in the USA: at Indianapolis and the new Circuit of the Americas, near Austin, Texas. Recent champions include Italian Valentino Rossi, who rides Yamahas, and Spaniard Marc Márquez, who rides Hondas.

| 300 | 400 | 500 | 217 mph |

FAST AND DIRTY

For thrills and spills on a motorcycle, little can beat American Dirt Track racing. The bikes race in close formation around a dirt track at speeds of up to 130 mph. But the dirt is so slippery that riders cannot simply bank around corners. Instead, they have to put their inside foot down on the track, sending up a shower of dirt that "roosts" the rider behind. That's why most riders wear a steel left shoe!

Top Speed | 50 | 100 | 200

POWER
Over 90 bhp

0-60 MPH
2.5 seconds

TOP SPEED
140 mph

ENGINE
Up to 1,000cc

TORQUE
Over 50 lb-ft

PRICE
Anything
from a few
hundred
dollars up

DIRT TO ICE

Dirt Track races take a variety of forms. The most popular is Flat Track racing, in which bikes race around a mile-long circuit. Speedway looks like Flat Track racing, but the bikes have no brakes, so riders put their feet down to gain control. Races can take place on grass (Grasstrack) and even on ice.

BARE BONES

Flat Track bikes are stripped down to the essentials. They are much lighter than road bikes, with much thinner tires. They have front and rear suspension, but brakes only on the rear wheel. The suspension is much softer and longer to allow the wheels to easily squeeze up over big ruts.

300	400	500	140 mph

DIRT QUICK

Dirt bikes aren't made for the fastest times along smooth, flat roads. But on dirt, bumps, and mud, they can jump, skid, and climb with astonishing speed and agility—and toughness. And when the way is clear, they can accelerate to speeds of up to 100 mph in the blink of an eye. What matters is low weight, good balance, and impressive pulling power.

LEAPING AND LANDING

To make jumps and soak up big bumps, dirt bikes need suspension with a lot of movement. They also need wheels that are easy to maneuver. So dirt bikes have much smaller wheels and longer suspensions than road bikes. Before each race, dirt bike riders "tune" their suspension to make sure it lands just right.

LIGHTWEIGHT AND NIMBLE

Typically, the fastest dirt bikes have two-stroke engines of about 500cc and weigh under 300 lb. Among the best known are the KTM 450 SX-F, which has a 44cc engine and weighs a featherweight 237 lb, enabling it to reach 123 mph. Other fast dirt bikes include the ATK Intimidator, the Kawasaki KX450F, and the Honda CRF450R.

Top Speed	50	100	200

POWER
53 bhp

0-60 MPH
7 seconds

TOP SPEED
123 mph

ENGINE
449cc two-stroke

TORQUE
34 lb-ft

PRICE
$10,199

300	400	500	123 mph

Kawasaki Ninja

The Kawasaki H2R Ninja's fairing is not just a glamorous piece of styling. It was developed in a wind tunnel. It not only keeps the bike streamlined to minimize drag, but also has little winglets that use the airflow to help force the front wheel down onto the road and improve grip.

Suzuki Hayabusa

Soon after the Suzuki Hayabusa became the world's fastest production bike in 1999, Japanese bike makers decided to artificially limit the top speed on all bikes to 186 mph. Although bikes could actually go much faster than this, they are prevented from doing so by the electronic control unit (ECU) that controls the ignition—the sparks that set the fuel in the engine alight.

Jet Power

The US Federal Aviation Administration insists that jet engines in planes must be retired after a certain time. But MTT, the manufacturers of the Y2K bike, realized there was plenty of life left in these engines. MTT recondition them and give them a new life in turbine-powered motorboats, fire pumps, and generators—and motorcycles—where a single splutter will not cause a calamity as it would in a plane.

Honda Blackbird

The smoothness and power of the Honda Blackbird's engine depends on its digital 3-D mapping computerized ignition system. This ensures that ignition (the spark that sets the fuel mix alight) occurs at the best possible moment. Conventional ignition systems vary ignition timing according to engine speed only. The Honda's 3-D system also factors in how hard the engine is working.

Lightning LS-218

The Pikes Peak International Hill Climb in Colorado is the second-oldest motor race in the USA. In one event, motorcycles compete for the fastest time up the grueling, twisting slope. In 2013, the all-electric Lightning LS-218 announced its presence in the world by a dramatic win here. The LS-218 stormed up the slope in almost exactly ten minutes—a full 20 seconds faster than the gas-engined Ducati in second place.

Ducati Race Bikes

Based in Bologna, Italy, Ducati are one of the major makers who compete in MotoGP, developing motorcycles especially to race. For these bikes, Ducati use their famous V-shaped engine layout. The V formation, with the two cylinders set at right angles to each other, allows the firing of the cylinders to be perfectly balanced, without the additional balance shafts that inline engines need.

INDEX

GLOSSARY

Brake horsepower (bhp) The power direct from the engine; 1 horsepower can move 550 pounds one foot every second, written as 550 ft-lb per second

Fairing The lightweight shield and windscreen at the front of a bike that streamlines it and protects the rider

Monocoque A body made from a single piece

Production bike A motorcycle made for sale in large numbers in a factory

Supercharger A device that boosts an engine's power by using the engine to turn a fan that forces extra air and fuel into the cylinders

Torque The force with which something turns, measured in pounds per feet (lb-ft)

Traction The proper grip of the wheel on the road for acceleration

Turbine A circular fan with a lot of small blades, or a jet engine that works a fan like this

Two-stroke engine A very simple engine in which the cylinders fire every second stroke, not every fourth as in four-stroke engines. Great for small, high-performance bikes.

THE AUTHOR

John Farndon is Royal Literary Fellow at Anglia Ruskin University in Cambridge, UK. He has written a huge number of books for adults and children on science, technology, and nature, and has been shortlisted four times for the Royal Society's Young People's Book Prize.

THE ILLUSTRATORS

UK artist Mat Edwards has been drawing for as long as he can remember. He began his career with a four-year apprenticeship as a repro artist in the ceramic industry and has been a freelance illustrator since 1992.

Jeremy Pyke left the RAF to follow his passion for illustration. He has worked on many children's books and uses oil, watercolor, computer-generated illustration, and 3-D animation.